The Wild Rose Asylum

AKRON SERIES IN POETRY

The Wild Rose Asylum

Poems of the Magdalen
Laundries of Ireland

Rachel Dilworth

WINNER OF THE 2008 AKRON POETRY PRIZE, CHOSEN BY RITA DOVE

The University of Akron Press
Akron, Ohio

All rights reserved ✳ First Edition 2010 ✳ Manufactured in the United States of America ✳
All inquiries and permission requests should be addressed to the Publisher, The University
of Akron Press, Akron, Ohio 44325-1703.

13   12   11   10   5   4   3   2

LIBRARY OF CONGRESS CATALOGING-IN-PUBLICATION DATA
Dilworth, Rachel, 1974–

  The wild rose asylum : poems of the Magdalen laundries of Ireland / Rachel Dilworth.

    p. cm. — (Akron series in poetry)

  "Selected by Rita Dove as the winner of the 2008 Akron Poetry Prize."

  Includes bibliographical references.

  ISBN 978-1-931968-61-4 (pbk. : alk. paper) — ISBN 978-1-931968-71-3 (cloth : alk. paper)

  1. Women—Institutional care—Poetry. 2. Institutional care—Ireland—Poetry.
    3. Reformatories for women—Ireland—Poetry. I. Title.

  PS3604.I4637W55 2010

  811'.6—DC22

                    2009041706

The paper used in this publication meets the minimum requirements of American National
Standard for Information Sciences—Permanence of Paper for Printed Library Materials,
ANSI Z39.48–1984. ∞

Cover: *Descending Angel* by John Wimberley. Used by permission.

The Wild Rose Asylum was designed and typeset by Amy Freels, with help from Amanda
Gilliland. The typeface, Mrs. Eaves, was designed by Zuzana Licko in 1996 for Emigre.
The Wild Rose Asylum was printed on 60-pound natural and bound by BookMasters of
Ashland, Ohio.

Contents

Foreword

Until 1996, and with origins dating back to 1767, residential institutions that came to be known as Magdalen laundries—also called Magdalen asylums, homes, and female penitentiaries—existed in Ireland. Taking their name from Mary Magdalen, Christianity's exemplar of female penitence and redemption, and from the difficult laundry labor required of inmates to finance the institutions, Magdalen laundries were facilities for the managed care, reformation, and containment of "fallen women."

A number of Ireland's smaller asylums, including its first, were run by Protestant lay people. But by far the largest and ultimately most controversial institutions were run from the mid-1800s onward by four female orders of the Catholic Church: the Sisters of Our Lady of Charity of the Refuge, Good Shepherds, Sisters of Mercy, and Irish Sisters of Charity. Early laundries focused on providing prostitutes, women who had been "compromised," and unwed mothers with temporary refuge and rehabilitation for Victorian society. Over time, however, and by early-to-mid years of the twentieth century, the nature of the convent laundry seems to have changed to feared and confining penitentiary.

By then, the counties that became independent Ireland contained ten convent laundries, most housing over one hundred (and some, one hundred fifty to two hundred) inmates at a time, not free to leave. Women and girls seen as morally deviant, at risk, or socially undesirable were brought by town priests, family members, nuns at other Church-run institutions, employers, officials, and court order. These women included a major subset of unwed mothers, in addition to teenagers merely suspected or thought in danger of sexual activity (for instance, due to "boldness"), victims of sexual assault and incest, women with mild mental challenges, women who had committed infanticide, prostitutes, and others considered vulnerable, problematic, or "bad." Most were confined without legal sentence, and women spent years in arduous unpaid labor, austere denial, and constant prayer.

Many women became so institutionalized, they were unable to function "outside." Others became so frightened of men, so scarred by lack of normal social relationships or loss of a child, they lived permanently damaged lives. Some have reported being victimized by men while in the asylums.

With social and other advances in later decades of the twentieth century, the laundries seem to have begun to change again, and one by one, they closed. Characterized until the 1990s by collective silence, the issue of the institutions is an extremely complicated one. So many women arrived at Church-run laundries already abandoned by families, lovers, or larger community. To date, historians have not been given access to the twentieth-century records of the convent laundries. The number of Irish women who passed through the institutions therefore remains unknown. There is a commonly used estimate of 30,000.

Author's Note

The poems in this book grew largely from my experiences of living in Ireland for a year, 1999–2000, to try to learn and write about the highly complex, sensitive, and disturbing issue of the laundries. What happened to individual women, and to so many collectively, moved me again and again beyond words; and it challenged me, as a woman and a person, to try to find my way back to them. These poems attempt to render different elements of what I took away and a sense of factors, perspectives, social mores, and experiences related to the laundries' existence. I surely acknowledge and respect that there are so many different personal experiences (many still remaining untold or unknown), feelings, and views among people who lived the reality and circumstances of these institutions, and in no way do I mean anything here to contradict the scope of that. Moreover, these poems were written by an American, someone who approached the subject in Ireland at a particular time, a poet not a historian; and for any ways that I may have seemed to err, I sincerely apologize. I know that I offer the poems as a woman looking at the issue of the laundries "from the outside," but I would like to say very genuinely, they were written in hopes of affirming that none of us is ever *outside* of a subject like this, and if we are, we are in the wrong place.

And I took all the blame out of all sense and reason,
until I cried and trembled and rocked to and fro,
riddled with light.
          —W. B. Yeats, "The Cold Heaven"

The Magdalen Laundries

I.

Laundry seems so benign, no real sentence
on its own—stress falling on the first syllable
with its gauzy vowels, its clean-rinse consonants.

The word doesn't sound like the scald and pound, the beating
of steam machines. It smells nothing like
fifteen-foot walls of stone scabbed with mold

or the rank stench of bleach, doesn't burn like sweat
and chemicals on newly opened skin.
Penitentiary is less misleading,

it calls up zoos and jailed collections: bestiary,
aviary. *Penitents*. That word
slaps at your mouth with the good hurt of church.

II.

They were *unmanageable*, these women.
A priest marked Chrissie early on: in moral danger
since she'd been orphaned. Clare was another matter,

she'd tried to run from home when her Da had come looking
for fun, juiced-up and mean. The Gardai caught her
the next day hitching out of the county.

It was drink chased Rose the months it rained
with Himself away hustling work, while lads in the lanes
came for Eve each day once her soldier'd moved on.

Mary and Annie were slow, saw life like tall children.
The other scores of penitents were stained
with the filthiest sins: heavy mounds of heart

and stirring blood, well-rounded evidence
of ash and dust, of flesh of one flesh.
They would never be clean again. Who could forgive this?

III.

No need for any name but Magdalen
so the others disappeared: Bridie, Kitty,
Maureen, Shauna, Medbh, Lizzie, Kathleen,

all gone. Best to purify the past
of the pull in recollection. Auburn,
chestnut, honey—all lopped off

with abrupt swipes. There was satisfaction in the rough,
blunt line of the first cut, in harvesting the vain
tresses, in bulby heads smudged with hair.

No thought of the rivering strands that had dried
the feet of Christ, no memory that red lips kissed Him,
that the Magdalen had washed God with her tears.

IV.

God, but I'd love to see her. You'd think
it was her fault, poor wee bastard. You'd think
she was death Himself the way they swept her off. Bleedin'
Sisters will tell her I'm dead, or left her somewhere.
They'll tell her that I never wanted her.

Ah Sheila, leave be. There's nothin'll come of that talk.
Listen to Deirdre now—I've a girl as well,
you know, in the industrial school. You've got
to not want her, pray Jesus you never see her,
'cause if you do, it'll mean she's one of us.

Body Sonnets
I. Credibility

So much yourself that even the river is you—
length fathomed as a curve that stirs the light,
muscles wing-swept and slow to be moved.
Your very name, *swan*, is absolute.
No part of you is mystery to itself,
not breast nor skin nor wind-delighting eye;
no impulse strange to you if seldom felt,
nor missed, nor lost with opportunity.
Time blooms in you. Whole evenings of milk-
weed and wet earth billow *new, new*
as your body makes its own white space, builds
a pure, relentless physical truth.
Credibility of light, you are the star-
clear argument that justifies the river.

Guarded

In care, she learned to guard against herself.
Against her saucy form, its dirty bits
pudging mutinously out: lips, bum, womb, tits.

And against her feebleness, her thick heart with its
baby hopes that love would sally in
the kip fish shop and like the look of her

despite the smell of haddock on her dress
and the ghostly scales that always littered her
nail varnish like wet petals. They took that,

first thing: her Kiss of Shine. Then, her frock with
the pin-prick posies went for soap-water wool
and a starch-stern apron that tamed her shape.

The pong of fish for bleach. Her name for a saint's,
or rather, another go, since your one hadn't taken
to her. (Just as well with the loads of other Marys.)

Her head of corkscrew porter-colored curls
was humbled to a speckled lump—a seed
dandelion blown—in case of nits, and as first penance.

Confused, she watched the rest go: her laugh,
her sense of time, the podge that had dogged her legs
since she was ten, her flair for song, her little one.

One night, even her father's face was gone
and she slipped in her bed without picturing his sheet-
white teeth or the raised mole under his breastbone.

Here, she was a new girl. She was in charge
of suitable things like mends, like blanching out stains.
No gutting of flesh. No semblance of a fishy past.

She found evident definition in walls, screened
safe from the huge blue night that bruised the world,
day in, day out—the awful con of the things beyond.

Grew to fear the bad job she'd always make of it
out there, the riot of life and its deceptions,
the rapaciousness of the homes and lanes

restrained by spikes and stranglings of wire.
Inside these grounds there was the surety of women
charged with caring for her—mothers and sisters

to school her into dreamless sleeps
and a correction in which it was to be possible
to forget she had, somewhere, a son,

and be, herself, a child again
with no sense of permanence: when a thing was gone
it did not exist. Perhaps had never been.

Like a memory unshared, she grew ever more removed
from her origins, from her first clear truths.
Year by year, she steamed, ironed, hemmed in—

to herself quiet days that let her give to God
the gift of clean sheets and silence: a good girl.
Only now, with her old age, is she jealous

of her few certainties: dislike of parsnip mash,
the wizardry of her cribbage game, and Tuesday morning
visits from pretty Bridget, the physical therapist

who comes armed with the scrapes of her gang: three lads,
one girl. There is some apology between them, a knowing
sense that things long gone aren't lost in the forgetting.

The young mum, on leaving, is always cagey
to the nuns, gives up nothing more than *Sure,
Joan is keeping fine. Sharp for her age, that one.*

The Cloistering of Mary Norris

Good Shepherd Magdalen Asylum, Cork, 1950—early 1953.
Entered age 17.

Are there stones of water on the moon?
Are there waters of gold?
. . .
Is it there that the drowned live?
—Pablo Neruda, "Planet"

I do not picture sheep anymore—
thirty, sixty, two hundred bounding
ceaselessly, magic-propertied
over wave on wave of stony wall.

For the birds, that. Rubbish.
My green mind forfeits no space to dreaming.
I am precious with it, fearful it become,
itself, a dream of what might have been.

I keep myself awake with words:
razor, puncture, mitre, claw.
Think of: the shards of bottles ripping atop
the convent wall—ramparts of glass

fortifying the brittle castle.
       Such a landing! for a sheep too great
       with flesh, or weak, or young yet
       for the strength to disregard the law

       of gravity, of physical properties. . . .
       Who *would* I be to risk a lamb
       on that? (It's not a leap of faith
       unless there's something to believe.)

The dormitory orders even
the night, shadows of bed on bed
catalogued like books on a shelf.
They are so easily read: uniform

lines and matter, lack of substance—
the same old story. (I am too bright
for this, for the blackening of histories
to plots so dark they seem the same.

Normalization is sleight of hand.)
Think: chicken white, fat vein,
soot plum, ocean, orange.
          I was mad for the pictures once. Had two

                    parents, then one. Knew the lift of the wind
                    off the grass, and a river. I lived on a farm.
So much just continuation
in these sleepy hours, each slowed breath

for someone else, for yet another
day weighed by labor, day fenced with silence.
          Confiscate the right to claim.
                              But oh,
          the machinery will not stop bleeding. . . .

Breathe out, breathe in. This is no dream.
Breathe out, breathe in. Carbolic, bleach,
must from the rug. No hob, no sweaty rowan.
Breathe. Breathe. Something my own.

I soft-toe to the loo, bolt myself in.
There is a clear cold off the lino
and a milky film of cast-off
light from the moon in the window frame.

A plump, pale turnip, the moon
roots in the chunk of heaven
the wall hoists up. I name this
mine: night's growing season,

the smooth and girlish round
line of the moon and the porcelain,
the rise of the wall to the high window,
the box of glass making its own space,

my tears, the rain awaited all day,
moments
                                    entire.
I feel the shape of each one—like a coin
in a trouser pocket, summed by touch.

A brush of my hand confirms the loot
stuffing my nightdress pocket—news
from the papers village women have used
to truss their clothes and table linens.

I try to find whole stories to save
from the bin in the sorting room. But
generally, the vital bit's gone missing—
the conspiracy theory or why of the riot,

the picture of the race meeting winner,
the price beef got to, or source of a crisis. . . .
At least I know the half of it. At least
I know exactly what I'm missing.

I carry the news with me like this—
against my body in the dark—so as to hold
the world close, to dress myself with nearness
to the strange, great variations of the self-made.

The depth of these hours feels good,
as when your hand, plunged far
down in damp earth, has reached the place
at which it can cup a plant by the roots.

On the floor of the loo, I set out rows
of articles and bury myself in a field
of names, voting, brides, sport.
I steep there, a seed or skeleton, beneath

the soft-lit eye of the moon with its hinterlands—
its daily-changing shape a talisman—
until I can feel myself bulging against the room's
straight walls, shoved by their trellising

edges up, until I am something bent
and wandering, striking out and out
to the high light, filling what space I find,
urging, asserting, *I am this*

big, this too is mine, I am this, and this—

The Heart of the Matter

My attention begins with the mantle of light that is everywhere and
    spectral, like snow.
Lambency drifts the garden, the back wall, the patio with a self-same

look of sensation. I step into air cold and awash. It feels like it is
    ringing,
like it can nothing but ring. It feels like astonishment. I glance up

and it is as though I have just been born, just arrived after a long swim
    to the cataclysmic
experience of breathing. The moon, the moon

is a coal, eye of hunting owl, an awful cell huge and near
and more—there is a hooped bruise aching the sky green around it,
    a whole region

of echo and increase. Oh, the world is round! It is *round*!
How have I never understood this shape before? And how is it
    possible, this

leviathan? What can be left of the rest of the sky?
What is left to protect us when such a thing as this exists?

The aureole is so far-reaching that it suggests the bloom of bomb or
    fallen
crown. But that as easily seems wrong,

and the moon not a cause but rather
a focus or distillation.

The more I look, the more looking becomes, itself, gargantuan
and I know this moment the most human—this stupefying

at what sheer bulk has not been imagined.
My sense dilates as I stare and staring fill

with imperative to be here, only here, to witness *this*,
to take it in and scatter it again, burn

so with the sight of it that *I* must be seen
as I call to the stunned rest:

I and everyone must never be the same again. This
is the revolution of being. This is the revolution.

Amazing Grace

I.

My mother's mother's hymn, the one that stunned
a dark, lush ache into the least of us—
me with my four years overrun
by what had seemed usual happiness.

My earliest association with death,
that hymn, and the curious, baleful
acceptance warming our kitchen
as my parents learned white blood cells had engulfed

someone I knew mostly as arms and the swish
of a moth-wing summer dress. (Later,
I'd learn that my unreasonable love of little
gestures others miss and holidays

were also hers.) *I once was lost, but now*
hums Mom the odd time, at large in the roses or dusting.
It is joy, I think, the fierce thing that grounds
tears from me but soothes her about that song . . .

the overwhelming knowledge of how small
our claim is on goodness; that *the free, unmerited*
favor of God (the dictionary's bald
elucidation of grace) is the awful easement we share;

that no mere person who loves could ever give
the refuge of raw, unaccountable Mercy.
Seductive beyond words, *that* kind of love,
hope which pullulates from seminal hurt.

Is that what breathed, what stirred, when you heard the world's view:
It is the grace of God that runs the refuge . . .?
What starling thing beat through the valleys of your face
after all those years of contemplating Grace?

II. Create in me a clean heart, O God

Convinced, you were, that you would get it right.
That you could learn, as though it were a skill
or trade, to draw His love: the Way, the Light.
That surely there was just some art or will

that hadn't taken hold in you, but would
in time. You clung to that: the master plan,
the seeming logic of your work. Believed "the blood
of Jesus Christ His Son cleanses us from all sin."

*Right enough, John, you thought; that means
He'll see me free of the comfort Mam took
in the pigman's talk, the gentle way of him
on a Thursday after nights of Da on the rip,*

*a pan in the face. (Sure, though, wouldn't you think
it'dve happened before I was brought here
from the Home? But then, love takes time to sink in. . . .)*
You took bright words to bed like *reward, fair*

play, and *liberty*, sure if you could only cozy
up with their warmth, they'd change the shape of your life
to something large and amorphous, *quelque chose*—
that phrase of Sister's you loved for its lack of contour.

But understanding that God favored ritual
mortification, you kept duly at this:
knuckle-scrubbing hotel sheets of tell-tale
stains, underthings from the men's prison,

sticky bits of guts off the aprons
of operating theaters and butchers' shops,
and the guttered blood and mucousy glops
of tissue out of sanitary towels from the women

in the trim little houses over the wall.
You were forever making ready for God
a place in all this. But at length, it seemed faulty
prescription—the endless *Our Father*

to eradicate your hard-and-fast family
lineage (like mother, like little one). It never
managed to afford you absolution
and by middle age, you had one same terrible prayer:

Good God, I've no love left to console
the pure bird heart I grew with tender care
to wait for you in this dank, windless place.

Lift it out of me. How dare you teach me "Grace
responds to the deepest yearnings of human freedom?"
Eloi, Eloi, lama sabachthani?

Research Piece:
"sub rosa"

sub rosa, *adv.* confidentially;
secretly; privately. (*Latin:* lit.
"under the rose," from the ancient
use of the rose at meetings as a symbol
of the sworn confidence of the participants,
from the legend that Cupid once gave
Harpocrates, the god of silence, a rose
to make him keep the secrets of Venus.)

Falling Away, *a pathetic fallacy*

"Falling away" was a colloquial term used in nineteenth-
and twentieth-century Ireland to refer to a woman's fall
from moral and spiritual grace due to sexual activity,
sometimes resulting in pregnancy, outside of marriage.

As a veil might, the finches fall
away from the birch in a soft release.

One and two and thirty leave
the young limbs on a drape of wind (piebald
bark goose-fleshed in the rimy light)
as each bird acquiesces to some right
pulse or breadth of breeze—or feasibly,
the broad-backed lure of solid ground—
and the "dumpy" body
ascribed it by the wild guide
slips driftingly to the sureness of earth.

There must be pleasure in this, yes; in the sound
thump of coming up against the stride
of the long land with its balance, its dumb girth.
And?
⠀⠀⠀⠀⠀⠀in reassurance of the bird's own flesh,
proof the spud-sized finch is not itself
a mere inconsequence of heights or
ornament of stature.

⠀⠀⠀⠀⠀⠀⠀⠀⠀⠀The image, indeed, of *easiness*—
this tender slide of plumping breast that flight
cannot quite imitate.

⠀⠀⠀⠀⠀⠀⠀⠀⠀⠀The graceful give
of it! The unexpected claim
on beauty in this declination,
in this movement more familiar, more
understandable than flight.

                    Like—
the skimming of a towel off the frame
of a niece's body before her bath
as she waits, singsong-eyed, for you
to wash her hair; next tumbling, her laugh.
Or,

          a trill's natural diminuendo
as it tenders on cue
to a stillness ripe with the glamour and swell
of the concerto's final echo.

Three months past, leaves would have moved
like this: poplar ships with yellow sails
furled dragging down-current a ways
to overtake land, at last.

                    Before them,
bulky late-summer
lumps of plums well-gone into the phase
of blushing much too red to reason
further bide of time.

                    Still,
for all their commonness, the birds seem . . .
what? *surprising* in the ground's low element.

What business have wings, after all, poking round
the undergrowth or puttering in the new
gang of firstling crocuses hell-bent
on stretching their soft spears up
and dredging the cold air for light enough to blot
the lawn with succulent small suns?

Body Sonnets
II. Death of a Maiden

It rose and rose from me, rapid and clear
and light as hot glass from the tip of a pipe.
It grew so beautifully, it had to break.

Vividness. The girl with the cracker-jack
grin, those lightning wings and a big-heart chest.
And yet, why would that heroine lose bloom

and sight of life's big come-on *in medias res,*
just as the story begins, begin again
to absence, embarrassment, and the loss (oh God,

who is writing this?) of a body dawning
long-fingered and flush as a lilac bush
to nothing greater than pure loneliness?

Who scripted *this* as an end more proper
than a one-off death, spectacularly Irish?

Body Sonnets
III. Island

They have shown us a portrait of Ireland
unclothed of towns: veins of stream, wrinkles
of mountains, skin freshened by rain, pale sand,
low realms of lough and stone. She is beautiful,

they say. I wouldn't know. Her figure's the first
I've ever heard so praised for its nature.
Even the bodies of saints aren't right till they burst
into flames or are cut to pieces—torment-altered.

Yet this breadth of grass and hill and coast defies
the shame of form although so lush, this she.
Why is such a woman loved yet I'm undone?

Looking long, I believe the white weight of sky
surrounding her the key: the acquittal of beauty
is in *island*.
                    I want to belong to someone.

Body Sonnets
IV. True to Form

Cursed is the ground for your sake.
—Genesis 3:17

Who wouldn't want to keep it covered up—
great lump of blood and bone, weepy as meat?
I'd have to be daft to be vain of form—that
doughy body of bulge, bilge, loll, and tear
flushing swine-pink at a little work or heat
and spoiling clean lines with bulbings like tumors.
Mad to imagine pulses might go a-gallop
at a havoc of chew-spit curls that will not stay plat
for all the bloody grass in Ireland.

It sickens me to think that I am this
and more, the seat of some gross ache I understand
not at all. But for the cavernous sense that I am accomplice,
I would not be tempted to think myself beautiful,
not like a fruit—the shape and taste of *apple*.

Body Sonnets
V. Composition

My body bears the story like a page
on which you are composed each day in verse.
In memory I find the means to pray
with faith again. So come, be written. First,
the hale and buoyant movement of your hands
like rills along my pulse, my skin; your voice
felt as blueness, its grit blowing like sand
on a dark dune; breathing *I love you by choice*;
the sense of touching you so like a rhyme,
a coming right again; your eyes my image
of wind and summering; your scent a line
to do with leaves; your grin the gist of moorage.
Forget, I'm told, and *Learn to be alone.*
But the womb's an inky thing: bloodripe, touchstone.

Body Sonnets
VI. Afterwards, the Other

How it seems so blatant and yes, too much to bear.
A white mirror. A gaze. A heart in crayon.
How the thought of it persists, obsessive as ghost.
How it moves like jeopardy, there and there. . . .
These the wielded, the instruments by which
I conceive desire a fiction of the helpless
and know myself nearly content alone,
beset by form but not acts or claim or niche.
Beneath its skin of hardened sun: flood
water rising, a course that can't be stopped.
I fold in and in, centering no man.
No governance again. I am aloft:
unseduced by confidence, the gleam
of touch, approval, the intimate, the dream.

Body Sonnets
VII. Escape

For Josephine McCarthy, who had been
"as green as the grass in Ireland."
Good Shepherd Magdalen Asylum,
Cork, 1961–64. Entered age 18.

A room that wants for light, is one long wall
turning and returning on itself
with all the convolution of a lie,
my body riddles me with bleak resolve.

If I am painted black, let me be starling.
Let me become the night stolen away.
Come dark and dark, hold you this beauty. Say:
"institution" can mean "the act of starting."

Stray painter's razor—A nun: "Well, do it then"—
begin the end, conceive the lure of option.
No passion bound me here. So, logic blank,
may its awful edge now cut me free again.

      The soul's a fire poppy. It will rip like skin
      to sticky life, insisting *open, open.*

Letters to a Girl on Leaving the Home

Now then, miss, it's fixed.
So let this be an end
to the pettish whine and carry on

you've been feeding the nuns.
Such a show—you with six months
plumping, bold as brass—over this

daft business of wanting
to keep it with us, as if we'd not
suffered your pleasure enough

with the heartbreak blood-
red of the pants hid in the bin
after your Mick's twenty-first.

And him with the hot eye for Boston.
Jesus. A head full of cheese
you have: nothing but hole.

How could you, my girl,
lay us open on the altar?
Take a flyer for a little trouser?

What matter. Done now
and no harbor but bargains.
Your father's organized a lad—

gone forty and not the full
shilling, but you'll take him, so.
He's a farm and no wife, and not enough

sense to care if his neighbors do
the math. Right. This keeps it decent.
Keeps mother and baby home

from turning into Magdalen
asylum for you, chick.
It's blessed you are with folks like us.

And if you're after thinking, He's half-
cracked! *What matters that?*
If when his fingers move on you,

they come from a rough place
or his whisperings froth as though
some sick barm, his glance unglued,

think how much better wed—
than padlock, what pummeling
of tongues would bolt your nights!

No one down the village likes
him, of course, so far gone off.
Let them fasten on that. "Mad-

man's wife" remakes you martyred
and so seemly again:
Fair play to her, taking her lumps.

You rail so, intent to beat
against his heart once more, at least
in namesake. . . . Strip

"bastard" of root and wing—
give yourself again
to cauterize the stain

of broken dream. My own: I wished
for you an otter's life—shore and river.
What did I know of the urge of current,

the pulse, the shudder of wind?
We wish for what we do not comprehend.
Striving searching course, wet life . . .

a surge of sun. . . . But I can't abide you
swelling up to drown the rest of us.
Every dream has an end. That's the bargain.

❋

    Time-riddled, what line can remit
    that in a month you will flood
    with that florid word, bloom with the pain

    of initial syllable, the ache of the second
    —*miscarry*—though already be bound
    into fearsome covenant for good?

Research Piece:
Entries in the Admissions
Books of the Magdalen Asylum, Leeson Street,
Est. 1767 for the Care of Young Protestant
Women After a "First Fall"

Ann Mechland, called Mrs. One:
August 17, 1767: Recommended by the Rev. Doc. Thompson.
July 7, 1768: Expelled for misbehaviour not conforming to the rules
of the house and supposed to be out of her reason at times.
>Gave her:
>a new stuff gown
>a box and lock to it
>paid for indenture and enrolling at the Tholsel in order
>to her going to America
>money
>Books:
>a new Bible
>Common Prayer
>Prep. for the Sacrament
>Dodriges Life and Progrefs of Religion
>Practical Knowledge of Religion
>four shifts
>a pair of stays
>two petticoats
>caps
>shoes and stockings

Mrs. Two:
Daughter of a widow in Sligo.

Margaret Langley, Mrs. Five:
Could read and write. Lived an exemplary good life for the eighteen
months, at the end of which time she was restored to her friends with
credit, who were ready to receive her with the greatest pleasure.

Elizabeth Gogan, Mrs. Six:
(fourteen months after entering) Her friends and relations would not see her, they thought she had best leave the kingdom. So at her own request left the Asylum to go to Maryland.

Mrs. Forty-One:
(after nine months) Eloped out of the street door about the dusk of the evening.

Five Images of Bliss

I.

I didn't know anything

Brothy life, body of water, how white
the eggshell makes you
look—white as an owl blazing
from a snowfield quick-
winged as a cry,
white as a dream of sand,
white as the cooked flesh of a fish.
Your shell cradles you, warm
and blank and paper-thin, holding you
tight, holding you in,
not understanding that while
there seems no need
for harder realities,
your heart is forming first
and will reach out, breaking
like day.

II.

about the facts of life and I didn't know that I would conceive or so on.

Like rain-soaked seeds or ships'
hulls made out of wood, her eyes
bloat with the drench of morning.
Lone, she is the epicenter of what light
remakes the street this primitive hour.

What is she doing here,
so far from her woods? Poor deer,

what original stupidity prevents anticipation
of the cars about to stream down
before you can run, the clamor
coming to the fair green, the hustling
commerce of the life of man?

It is almost impossible to imagine
this animal: so new
that she has not yet learned
to begin with fear, so new
that the unknown can seem,
indeed, just wonderful—

so much so that she is enthralled
in an amazed exchange of attention with the first creature
she encounters here and does not perceive

that the young farmer crossing town
who is eyeing now her sleek neck,
now her ears that cup sound like open palms,
her thick pink tongue just visible,
the tight design of her flanks and those matchstick
legs intended to kindle flight
and yes, her tremendous gift
of appearing and waiting so perfectly
still as though only for him,

is praising his miraculous luck
at finding her here, and first,
and is wondering if he just might be able to run
for his gun.

III.

I stayed with him, and he said he loved me.

Virginal gardenia,
billow of petals,
every touch remains with you.

IV.

He said that this was the only true way to show that you loved somebody.

Sweetheart, what big eyes you have.
                The better to see you with, my love.
And oh, what big hands you have.
                 The better to hold you with, my love.
And oh, what big teeth you have.
                The better to taste you with, my love.
And oh, what a dream is love.
                My dear, the better to have you with.

V.

And I met him again then, and he said, Well, you did it before; why can't you do it now?

Down the ashy corduroy of the dusk sky
as water down the slope of a gradual hill,
the pigeon slides, dips, spills
low and yet further until she has returned,
giving herself tenderly
to the gape of the coop awaiting her,
expectant. Then hopeful,
she turns once more to see the smile of the man
who is closing the door, who is murmuring
and reaching out to stroke
a finger down the softness of her breast
approvingly, well pleased.

And that was the time I got pregnant.

Mad Song Stanzas for a Coming of Age

One of illegitimate birth shall not enter the congregation of the Lord;
even to the tenth generation
none of his descendants shall enter the congregation of the Lord.
—Deuteronomy 23:2

The washed and sailing reeds
    are all the beard I grow.
        Slack flux my blood
        gone brown from good.
The canal is drifting slow.

I hardly had a body,
    so new it was to me—
        water much more
        my home than air
or breast, or company.

And so it was a giving
    back, a restoration,
        that brought her here
        midst full moonglare
in this most bitter season.

Almost as though she thought
    she could return me thus
        from whence I came,
        she put me in
burlap, then channel's course.

She moved as down the aisle
    of a long and silent church—
        swaddling from toes
        to crown . . . then close
of bag round stone . . . then lurch.

But I heard as I fell fast
       to sleep in a silty bed,
             her voice lift warm
          as if it bore
     a last blown kiss. It chanted,

Now you will travel far
       from here in a blue, blue dream
           and a gown of salt
          on the lull of small
   winds, and will be redeemed.

She said it many times,
       slowly and with great care
           repeated it—
         that desperate
   and lonely child's prayer.

Persistently it lapped
       and washed over me anew
           as I sank and sank
           and drank and drank
   that dream of the bluest blue.

And suddenly there was
       no bag, no stone, no sin
           and I was free,
         wet-glistening
   but she could not conceive

of me as pure beginning.
       I patiently observed—
           she kept her eyes
         trained on the rise
   of air, the bubbles' stir

and then, their quieting.
       Her mouth moved on—the words
         a mindless hum,
         a repetition
     so like the beat of birds

abandoning, intent,
       an unforgiving climate.
         Then finally,
         she let words be
    and grew content with silence.

And through that silence passed
      echoes of every shun
        and stone they'd cast
        upon our past
    and in the end just one

ghost remained to stare
      out from her deeps: a face.
        Then she turned and walked
        and as I looked
    her step fell into place.

Research Piece:
Conversation Regarding the Counseling
Helpline FAOISEAMH, 2000

Faoiseamh is a breathing out—
that first syllable a gust
of release in Irish.

The word approximates "relief
from anxiety, worry, and pain."

The sister tenders with cupped hands
as though a cold clean drink, *broken
humanity* as we speak of the old system.

Thousands of calls, so many returning at last
to industrial schools, to canes
and rapes and leather straps; but others
to dread of men or open space—whole roads
erased in the wild girl asylum.

I ask, any from men bereft
of women disappeared in care—
their old sweethearts, soldiers, bosses,
whispering, *There was a child. . . .*

The lay woman shakes her head. Such men
have not called for *Faoiseamh*, for relief
from anxiety, worry, or pain.

Season's Greetings

Sour sloe-fruit blue
and huge as nine tigers.
A proper sky today, a bloomer,
chats Breda—braided and bowed
and just gone six—swinging
her mum's free arm into pendulum.

Hocus pocus, a kiss
for every crocus. Pucker up,
Buttercup. Look at the rooks
soldiering, wings prissed in
and not a bit of song—
hard old birds. Or

maybe they're afraid, poor things.
Yesbird, nobird, scaredy
crowbird. Know why
the measle spots on cowslips
smell of pickle in the spring?
The sun's *curing* them!

Breda buoys like a robin
up the rutted path. The span
of the convent grounds, spreading
fabric of grass and trees and the like,
has her all wound. She awaits
this day regular, shored up

with her father's glass cases of meat.
Here there is the smell of sun
and animals still living: calves and sows
and hens fussing round the outyard,
great white as their own eggs.
And the only red is the steam-blush

cheek of the girls who pray away
the stains on her Daddy's aprons.
So rare to glimpse them, but today
mum's to wait in the ironing room
as Sister fetches last week's sheets.
Breda thinks the convent Laundry exotic:

smoking and long as a baddy dragon,
a-buzz with a swarm of no-see-ems.
Even the walls sweat. Nun distracted,
Breda is the star attraction and hesitant
smiles petal, bouquet from clumps of girls
at work tables. Two her neighbor Aoife's age

drift near—conspirators—to praise
her foal-sheen plaits, her ribbons, her name.
She likes them, likes the way
they admire her like she might burst out
in bloom right there and then, decides,
It should be this way more often.

She tries to catch the brood of rabbit eyes
that skitter to her, fright, spring back
to heavy rollers that flatten clothes like dough.
Breda giggles at the thought of making scones
from the vestments going through: they're stiff enough,
and wouldn't that make mass inviting?

The nun sails back on the boat
that is her hat. In this hulk
of a room with smokestack for mast
and so few windows you'd think
you might drown if you opened one,
the hat itself is a light, whitening against stone,

looking like wind. Breda imagines
the sea dreams it must give—Bombay,
New York, Tahiti, maybe even Rome.
Knows if it were hers, she'd cast off
again and again. Mum shifts and Breda ventures
a last look: a brief contention.

Mind the snowdrops, fresh as bells.
Mum, on a day like this, inside's not on
for love or money. *Choices, pet,* is all she gets
as she registers a tartness of grass
and the drift from the cows about, christens spring
out loud: *broom, bunch-of-keys, forget-me-not.*

Research Piece:
Correspondence from "Mrs. Mahony"

We came to live in Forster Street in 1950 when I was two years old. . . .
The terraced houses [on what was known as Magdalen Terrace] were
all occupied by families and we were allowed play in the field behind
the houses which belonged to the Mercy nuns. . . . We played there all
the time, making play houses, playing camogie, crude tennis and
cricket with a hurley and tennis ball. Until the early 1960s, Mr. [ ]
delivered laundry throughout the city driving a horse and dray. Every
evening he brought the horse into the field through a side gate. . . .
There was one tree in the field. I do not ever remember seeing a leaf
on it. It was a gathering place, a shelter and anything our imaginations
made of it.

❄ ❄ ❄

One family in [ ] had a housemaid who had been brought up in
Lenaboy, a daughter of the family is a friend and in fact I remember
this girl, i.e. the maid. The woman of the house noticed this girl who
was about 18 developing varicose veins and she was developing these
veins because she was pregnant. She was taken to the Magdalen Home
to await the birth of the baby, which was taken from her of course.
Afterwards she was again taken into the Magdalen Laundry, where
about a year later she again became pregnant! It was never known who
fathered the children and I daresay she spent the rest of her life in some
Magdalen Laundry.

❄ ❄ ❄

I often dream of that place I grew up in, the seesaw of the perfect
freedom of the Magdalen Field and the prison of the Laundry
balanced by a terrace of houses running parallel with the road
leading out of Galway.

A Bildungsroman for the Lads

I.

Hushy in the monotone he uses for Our Fathers and sums,
the slow mantra begins: *bitch, bitch, bitch*.

She doesn't hear him, or at least appear to, but has become
    distracted, he can tell,
by Michael hemming the double-callbox with his thrashed
    blue Schwinn.

Asshole's only nine. No fucking way he wins.
Short-dicked, grinny-faced fuck and his bike.

Operator, I want to place a call to this—he takes to it now with the
    full-on determination
he used to learn his drum solo, convince his mum he hadn't
    watched Ms. Mackenzie dressing

and last week, scare the shit from that pudding-eyed
    college chick
when he crept behind her on the trail and grabbed
    her ass—*fucking bitch*.

Stupid . . . fucking . . . prick tease . . . fucking stupid
bitch twists tight and hard on his tongue

then with squeaking enthusiasm, springs
from under his breath like a stiff metal bedspring.

Jesus! He shoves past fat-faced Mike who—
appreciating triumph—has squashed inside the box to bask

and giggling outright with the splash of the thing,
looks back to glory in the gape (*burn, baby, burn!*)

she turns on him like a slim little salmon and because he can,
because in that moment there is no beauty like the exquisitely
    apple-crisp newness in him, he grins

cunt

as he starts to sprint, trailing a flurry of elbows,
flailing, hell-bent, towards a taut and pretty ribbon.

II.

The shivering, pasty light
inside the bus keeps us
content with silence. By rote,
storefronts tick off, dim
and bruise the new green
of the deepening sky.

Open late, a beauty parlor sparkles
the blue promise of *NAILS*
as the neighboring pork butcher closes,
a glimpsed valentine
smudge of pinks. Stubby
hydrants, like thumbs

the sidewalk's grown for no good reason,
flag down dogs, distracting them
from the busyness of their evening walks.
Now and then, a Garda car strolls by.
The park wells up, turns
into housing. Lamplight blinks on.

Two boys in the back force the only
conversation: a monologue from the pale one
gangling by the window. *Julie*, scoffs Sprat,
the word itself a breathy laugh, *I fucking hate her.*
There are so many things wrong with her
that could be fixed. Her voice—Jesus God,

who could stomach the thing, all bitch whistle;
and skin spangled as a Yankee flaming flag. . . .
She could lose a few, too, couldn't she, fucking
fatso (there is laughter now from the stumpy one).
And sweet Jesus, her teeth . . . her fucking teeth . . .
I just want to punch them till they're straight.

The bus swings past the garage, two Spars, the Book
Nook and the boys get off, full of limbs
and the plastic swish of Umbro clothing.
It is deep fall, and the bit of night
their leaving lets on will not be warmed. By morning,
even the affable lights of the housing estates will be frozen.

III.

Thready seedling stars, pale-flushed
some shade of baby-toe,
dust the weeding college pitch
that hasn't seen a hurley match in weeks.
Over Easter holiday,
no one's around to see things right.

Blessed, thinks Lizzie, *silence to read*
as she wallows in a passion of grass.
There is nothing, your one imagines,
quite like the midday grip of sun
on your neck under a gush of hair,
that warm widening of time against your skin.

Then abruptly, she gives over messing
with bits of poems and reapplies herself to *discourse*
and *the dialogue between agency and self-as-construct*
as constructed by her UpDiv text and its free-verse appendage.
There is little wind, and her hot back
begins to dampen. A benignly leggy

bug commences a slow expedition
down the arc of her foot. Hedge leaves bristle
a little, quieten. Her eyes swing
to the top of a new page and she is reading:
Nike, Reebok, Adidas, Air Jordan
on a sudden circle of dingy leather and nylon.

Christ, she thinks. *Oh Christ. I didn't hear them*
coming. Holy God. A slow moment spreads
How could I let this happen between confusion
and panic in which there is nothing but sun—
the hot friendliness of the world percolating
outside of us, indifferent and large

beyond words. *Slut,* says one; *look at her,*
she wants it: she's already lying down.
At some point between her scream
and their scattering—they are sweet sixteen
and not yet ready
to see it through—the sweaty sun busts up completely

and the hulk of each boy's young body burns
into negative: the image of a man among men.
They spill back into the brush, satisfied
there is power printed in their gawky bodies, satisfied
that the woman they left is picturing them
still, is framing in her mind

the awful possibilities.

Wild Fuchsia

Like a firestorm, the way it blooms
red and pouring:
atmospheric phenomenon.

There's something about it
not to like. Perhaps it is
that way it sharpens the air.

Four blushy sepal blades apiece,
the drip of the eight stamens,
amaranthine heart, gravity.
Who wants to be made so aware?

There is also that sense
of the impossibly pretty thing
that cannot be overlooked.

Fuchsia, do you know yourself
this bold?
Can you hear the river
racing through your name?

What *should* one do,
after all? It really mustn't be
touched. O ruinous.

And yet,
one can't but understand
how hard it is to resist
exploring
such beauteous profusion,
handling just the tip
of one bloodshine petal.

But the bruise
of silk? Will one's own hand
be stained?

Filament, anther, stigma, style—
such an intricate system
of parts; they can hardly
have commenced without intent.

Do you know yourself
fashioned to covet birds,
to encourage? Your color
the wine of every bee?

Let go, you may overrun
the counties.

Too loose and ever-new, your bloom,
the way you slip into flower—
(there is something not to like)
a luxurious contagion.

Let us have the management
of hedgerows. You will make the most
glorious walls, blazing
beauty is in the orderly line,
the live fence, the palisade!

The strictures of defense
can be handsome.

In every county, you will
come to illustrate the link
between barrier and beauty.

Tumult of loveliness and the pull
of calyx and flush
and spreading shrub
that roots in the poorest of soils,
we will cultivate with care
the wilderness of your nature.

Awakening

It feels like watching a veil of rain turn
into the firs, the sails, the pile of leaves
by the coal shed in a wide night wind.

Fragments of the Shattering Glass

I.

It is ritual and Bible-based—the scapegoat
made to disappear
in the obscurity of a wild wood
bearing all the iniquities of the people
on its nubby, emblematic head.

❋

Imagine, then, the truth
bewildered to a story
not linear but holey,
as full of truths as your own child
is full of truths
and of evasions.

❋

The quick, clear eye
of all you did not do.

❋

Blame: a coin, a lackey, a hand-me-down.

II.

Now: there is gunning for nuns,

jumping ship
as the rudder flounders, the craft adrift
in intractable deeps of light.

: renouncing the women
who believed *In pain you shall bring forth*
and all the burns from a sleever
some part of making a clean slate,
who were there at the deaths of the nameless
but put bodies in the earth without a trace.

"The nuns" seen as a body even, not singly
people in their actions, led, coal-tempered, or kind.

: The disposition to forget
this kingdom of God's is a bird
with one eye looking up and one gone blind.

✳

And there is always the act of inception.

A woman rang me up with, *The Protestants
were at it, too. Leeson Street, where our maid went,
you know.*   The first,
Victorian *asylums* for the corrupted, "the feminine,"
penance, "social evil," excise of past. And "reform
and release," work to character, simpler size.

I write it. But what other words—
uniform? equivalent?

✳

There is, of course, Rome.
With the new millennium, the *purification of memory*
covered two thousand years of Christian *acquiescence* to sins
that had *injured the dignity of women. Humiliated. Cast into the margins.*
Acquiescence, the Crusades, the Inquisition. God,

what we Christians have done
that regret be our purity.

✿

You can just picture her whip of a father
righteous at the fence, railing in front of her siblings,
You'll not come into this house. You've disgraced us.
You can't be right in the head. . . . They'd say down the pub,
Good man to give the baggage her dressing down.
He did what he could for the family name.

Harder to envision
the wrist-width, the beef and heft of the belt
exacting a father's fear on the back
of a favorite, seen by her sister
chatting with a soldier at the gate.
The urge of the hide as it speeds to impact
untouched flesh, the contact of the buckle
with soft knobs of spinal column.
The rise of welts like a nest of red snakes
terrifying her skin, remain. She'll not live *outside* again.

Impossible, in truth, to conceive
of the trip from County Roscommon to Dublin—
the openness of fields, the ice-cream lambs,
the grass rain-bright—as a fourteen-year-old girl
is transported to a home for the wayward
after telling relatives of her cousin
and the farm fair, the stench of drink off him during
the "indecency" of the assault. Sure, no such talk
could be let round the village. Unthinkable, that.

Again and again, "You must try to understand—
the family is sacrosanct in Ireland."

✿

And you—
you who say, *This is not my story.*
My linens are warm in the press. My parlor is clean.
I care. I am a decent person—

What of

Mind yourself, miss,
or it's off to the nuns you'll be packing.

Those girls deserve what they get, man-mad,
semi-mental. Too bold for anybody's good.

The tea-and-biscuit whispers,
the habit of the intake of breath: *God,*
isn't it desperate? and the reflex of hailing
a pal with, *C'mere, what's the scandal?*

No black-and-whites on the wall of the bank
showing the scepter of a smokestack mounting the town
from the old home for unwed fathers and lads at risk
of copping to the gist of randyness and the appeal of women.

You—
you with the tidy town and the storied
walls full of wide-eyed windows,

you with the children who played in the field,
the mass cards, the dirty sheets, the good hearts,

how did all of this go on

and on?

Who is responsible for the beginning?

Her Last Immolation

Considering that, all hatred driven hence,
the soul recovers radical innocence . . .
she can, though every face should scowl
and every windy quarter howl
or every bellows burst, be happy still.
    —W.B. Yeats, *A Prayer for My Daughter*, June 1919

Can you feel it, Lord, the fissure moving through me?
Can you feel the breakage taking on its life, gaining speed, hastening
let go, let go at all your seams and give
finally, give way.

Did it begin with you? Have you sent me this
permission, this invitation, as a kind of gift?

I feel you near, Lord, feel your breath
as though you're near enough to take my hand.
Your breath is cool, cool as the mountain run-off
I used to bathe in as a child, cool as the wind.

I want to swim in you. I remember doing so
when I was young, when I envisioned you
in everything. How easy then, remember?
Easy the reach, and the gentle reception.

No hurry then. No movement gaining head, swelling forward, urging
        for the love of God
or alter-movement binding me in place
with child hands, soft and grasping, with murmurs
of moons and dolls and things *(ah mam, ah love)*.

How did I find my way to this, to a strangeness
where I feel each day like water under rock?

Am I a well, Lord, or a stagnation?
If I spring from my skin, will I lift into beauty
once again, feathered, natural as rain?

✳

So hard. I do not see myself in glass
anymore—in sun-dashed windows, in mirrors.
I see myself in stone. I am so strong. (Do others see
a woman?) I make no shards. My fissure runs,
purposed from within.

✳

It is the need to separate myself
into brightness, recreated
in Your own image. Mine, I give
away   *give way*—

They'd have me fashion men from it, and more, a girl
again. Perfect carbon. This state they want, I am
to raise it, Lord, the rock, the wing.

                              Even now,

it is all still written: "By her life within
the home, woman gives to the State a support
without which the common good cannot be achieved."

                         Gives to the, *give*—

so calm and fresh, the bath of your nearness,
the still pool of your hand.

In the fifties, they resolved mothers' "refrigerator" nature
—some female chill—was cause of child autism.
Schizophrenia. Hysteria: womb in very name.

How responsible we were. And still
the sum, accountable, of parts. I love them
so, Lord, my little petals, my husband,
love them with the furious yielding
of a long night's snow, blank and tender as awe.

The yield swells and quickens, rupturing—

it will not sustain the shadow-lipped insistence
that presses close and close these many nights,
dreamingly, hotly, intimating I resent
my own. God   this breach—

taking on the rush, slipping out, giving out, *giving way*
to the pressing on, the sure and certain urge itself
is such a weight, a dreamlike gravity, indulgence
now the tenderest form of new imagination.
                                              "Fracture"
is wrong with its sharp division. "Split," too simple.

This is the pressure of the unfathomed fault.

Beyond the kitchen window, You are wide
swaths of violet and ginger allaying
every nervousness. Such dusk! Such imminence!
I must be closer yet, move forward, be inside
the comfort of the garden light falling and falling.

I step out of the house. I move like love—
slow, and slow, and *slow*, and all at once
I smell the coming moon on the jasmine, white
lilies' opening, wind through the fruiting trees
and need nothing so much as nearing this
one loveliness, acting in sympathy—myself
the lift of stonechat to branch, the sweetening
tomato, the brown moth, the blackberry's droop, the cool
wetness of gas, the hot breath of the pivoting sword.

Oh Rose—His Dark Secret Love

does thy life destroy.
   —William Blake, "The Sick Rose"

I. The McColgan Case

Sophia McColgan was sexually and physically brutalized by her father for fifteen years, from the time she was six. Her siblings were also abused. He was sentenced to 238 years in jail, but with terms to run concurrently, a total of twelve years. With "remission," he was released in 2004, after serving nine years.

Her body shines like ice with the sweat of him.
He moves once, twice. Again. She wakes and wakes.

His breath bucks and shoves all over her
face a gamy fug. Like he's heaving boulders.

It is not light out at all. The evenings
have grown so long that he keeps the lamp dim.

In the dirty glow from the oil, she can see her breasts
rattle, the farm muck and pelt on his whaling torso.

Watch, he warns, and pastes her cheek to the floor.
The eyes in the ruptured glass are hers, are hers.

The mirror's a puzzle: what should be clear is not,
yet is unmistakably the image of breaking.

His rancor takes such life with each movement—
the air is pushed from her till her mind is light.

Death, she thinks, will come like a paladin
on a charger; I will be bodiless.

The cracks in the looking glass call out, *Slip through
and through—come away—no entry but this—*

Inside the glass is chatter, casual laughter,
girl-plucked petals: he loves me, he loves me not.

Inside the glass, she walks down the path
in a swishing dress. Goes to a dance. Spins.

A question is cracking through. A fog of pain.
Spinning, spinning, she starts to feel sick.

The jagged glass rips her as she is pulled back
whispering, prayerful, *There's no place like home.*

II. The Kilkenny Incest Case

> *For sixteen years, beginning when she was ten, the victim suffered extreme sexual
> and physical violence at the hands of her father, who sired his own grandson. In
> 1993, the father received a prison sentence of seven years.*

Like a brook trickling in weeds, cheeky with moon.
Your little bird sang while I choked her, he said.

The Alsatian pup did not as he took a slash
hook in the cerebellum. Oh God of the meek.

What must the powerless know of love?
Think feather, say down. Care not overmuch.

He was good at keeping his kingdom with him.
Putrescence of sheep and poitín and cigarettes.

Like a pack of smokes: *I want a bit of sex.*
Else: to flog out some climax: a lesson.

He'd not let it be questioned—young girl knocked up,
no fella and all. *Out whoring. Mad for the goods.*

The gravid months were awkward to maneuver,
but a real man will surmount obstacles.

The job of father, he found, required tools: steel
boot tip (right eye, groin), lump hammer, Polaroid.

Never suffered any bra burning in his house.
No sir, he got to the root. Lit the breast itself.

Oh, such passion for the literal:
Set the girls on fire, boyo. Make 'em scream!

Soft mammae, delicate snowdrops,
how can anyone protect you from yourselves?

Can we who have said *fire* for desire conceive the scent
of breast on candle flame, on cigarette?

She allows it must have been his need for youth
again—the hunting down, the taking of spring.

III. Case Reported in *The Irish Times*, July 22, 2000

> *A forty-four-year-old man pled guilty to three counts of raping his partner's
> learning-disabled teenage daughter, who subsequently became pregnant. His
> sentence was suspended on the condition of good behavior for seven years.*

Not right. All her life, it had betrayed her like a scar.
She didn't understand, but it was *her.*

It was: believing: the world hand-painted, words
cryptic pictures, "grin" the name for moon.

The best of praise: to be held close. It was
obscuring of what was wrong; connection.

He worked like a virus in the system,
muscling the path of least resistance.

(How little we protect what we do not see
as our doing. Miscreated innocents!)

Inconsequential. Oh, the word feels bodily—
and too big for *not enough* and *without reprisal.*

IV.

Red as cuts, as cheeks perspiring,
these blooms startle the bush that yields them.

Tacitly broke open. Burst and burst.
How could a blossom become so raw?

By definition, sweet and easy
bruised. Needy. New. Beautiful.

Hemmed with thorniness: *Ah, that's just them.*
I wouldn't like to be meddling. A family affair.

No voice sizzling the leaves, *I have surely seen*
the affliction of my people. . . . I have come to deliver them.

Research Piece:
Notice in *The Standard*, January II, 1935

The Magdalen Asylum, Lower Gloucester Street

The charitable are asked to kindly remember the above institution.
It shelters one hundred and twenty-five penitents
who pray several times daily for their benefactors,
living and dead.

Kimberlys on the Number Seventeen

Today, they seem medicated.
There is none of the hysterical
bombast of last week.

No sign that the young one
with the nutsy perm
will reaggravate conversation

with the, apparently three,
folks who kibitz with her
"up top." Not a peep.

And nothing but worry
from the yeasty-cheeked man
who, last time on the bus,

kept egregiously hollering
in gay, self-syncopated rhythm:
Doughnut! Dough-NUT!

His friend with the hiccup
eyes, led in by hand,
won't hazard a glance around.

She's well aware, today,
that everyone is watching—
that it's them sneaking peeks,

rather than the flip way round
of last week when, belle-like,
she cornered them in her compact

for whole seconds: *I see you*
bookworm, Thumper, pretty boy
in fuzzy jumper. You are mine.

Oh, but everyone fosters a collective
interest in windows . . . except for
the impossible old woman with arid hair

who assumes the right to look
for reassurance: *Poor dears,*
God bless 'em. They're on the bus!

Imagine. How far we've come,
everyone thinks, they must be getting off
soon, soon. For God's sakes, Granny

Gumdrop with the dumb plum rinse,
conform! Cease this looking around
searchingly, you ninny!

God knows your lot
kept them tucked up tight
like Kimberlys in a tin

only dutifully produced for callers,
instead of out for a spin
to the park, to the shop, to the pictures.

But Granny won't stop, she's lost
in the wonder of this,
in the whole staggering newness

of inmates on the city bus.
Granny, Granny, you are all of us.
We perch in your sugary hair

to watch. We duck behind you.
We are your shadow.
They, too, are uncomfortable

in the front seats. You can see it
in their shifting feet, their heads
shying to the side.

No, not like last week.
Someone has clearly reprimanded
their performance as nondecorous—

inappropriate for the bus,
this business of kibitzing, flirty peeps,
and certainly, any exhortation of breakfast.

Your one with the mad perm
and the head friends
seems so very young . . . her body

pretty as a fierce chrysanthemum.
She's a kind of romantic
image of the wild mind

kept quiet—beautiful
with anger and that tiny smile
of apology that is not for us

but the wonders in her head.
She's chagrined at exposing them
to our unruffledness . . . or

maybe the medication. Granny Goose, dear,
can we blame you? Who could trust her
with the world, with crowds of men

and women hungering only for normal
proportions? Trust her not to fracture
any further, splinter into a greater

number of hurts? We know too well
that tucked up in her exquisite silence,
those shattered selves wound easily

as they eat us slowly, quietly alive.

Seasonal Villanelle on the Location of My Summer Flat in Forster Place, Forster Street, Galway (former site of the Magdalen Home)

Cold as a well it begins, that time of wager
on the best in us. Long home by December First,
I struggle still to consummate my labor.

Perhaps it's hammy, just cinema to say (or
think) the uncanny house-hunt (for what it's worth,
that *cold* as well . . .) is reassurance of a wager

made purposely, some show of favor—
more explicit than creepy—for the gist of the work
I struggle still to consummate. My labor.

I summered on that place—wrote, talked, read, prayed for
(God, *summered!*) a way to the center, to gently burst
the cold defense: *Well . . . just the times, I wager.*

Better left, friends dubbed the chance to stay there.
Frightening. Morbid. To refuse the gift, far worse.
Nearness to struggle, the still heart . . . that, consummate labor.

It's become more intimate, the need to say, *The "four-star
holiday homes" next door are new,* write *disposed of, cursed
into the cold.* . . . The lucent need to wager
on untold others, on struggle, and still, on miracle—

The Glass Lake

Some impressionist has rendered a girl lake-gazing
for the cover art. A bonnet rimmed with primrose
ribbon waving in the unseen breeze. Her back is
gently turned, legs bare, sundress mirroring the lake's palette
of green and violets, beryl and forget-me-not. A kind of soft
come on in, suited to the "intimate" and "spellbinding."

But I am ahead of myself, jumbling the sequence
of events, starting with the end. *Come on in.*

Hardly shy or frightened, Niamh offers *her* room to show
"Sister's friend" (it is me this time) the way of things.

My first impression is of sentinels choreographed
toward the door. *These are my teddies,* she bursts, running
a crinkled hand down the back of one. Her whiskery lip turns up.

Her walls differ from the woman's downstairs, no pin-ups
of Mother Theresa, Jim Carey, Cinderella, or Christ to landscape
humanity, but bloom: a secret garden fashioned in art class
of the barest posies and watery broad-strokes of dawn.

Waves shake through seascapes the colors of a first party dress.
Clumps of roses and clover, stick-figure oaks, something like mums.

The model in the photoclock has not been tossed. The old
wireless looks ready to hum. I know its voices, when they come,
will be amethyst and green like the heather in the garden.

She maps the space, touching things: duvet here, lamp
there. Yes, I think, this could be a destination.

I'm into music, she divulges suddenly, waving off
the small stack of Sidney Sheldon, a Catherine Coulter
boasting histrionic pirate lovers. . . . *I haven't use for these.*

There is a calming of time, a sargassoing, here in this room.
She grins as if we've a secret—*Would you like one?*—
and submerges into gaze. Decides: *The Glass Lake.*

I can't like the risk of reducing this place
with its baker's dozen bears, one lamp, floribunda
in crayon, single window and chair. *But you might—*

No, I won't be wanting it. I won't read it: it's too thick.

Too thick a prettiness: all painting and spine and vernal miss.
Oh this is the one. This girl, she looks and looks—
what is she thinking? What does she see in the still blue pool?
Does she see it nearly broken—mishmash of bits in bruise hues—
yet with the forgiveness of perspective, a best-drawn thing?

Does she see how the soft parts of lake indicate depths
of perception, how she begins to take on the nature
of the object as she watches, turning verdantly blue?
How there is the matter of reflection? Is she contemplating
jumping in, or wishing herself bird enough to dive far
into the heart of it and bring up something?

I must, so delicately, take.

But in the wide bloom of iris, the mystery of her gaze, I see
that I am all wrong. This is not my statement to make,
and the close of my hand on the book is just to illustrate

the extent, the maturation of this unfathomed
female whose actions mean *I give
part of me to you, that you may recognize*

the still life can sometimes be enough.

Research Piece:
Phone Call Following My Letter in *The Irish Times*

Today it is a merchant's son from the northwest islands—formal, ninety, full of his age—who is unhappy with "this business." Such hubbub. His call begins, "Why don't you tell me what it is you hope to hear."

Brother to Mary Magdalen—Good Shepherd nun from the thirties, made head of a laundry as her father's daughter—he wants to say, "She was a very human person." He wants to say, even suspicious Mrs. Roosevelt was impressed on passing through in '42. And that some years back, a smartly got-up woman came to find him in tribute to Sister's kindness.

"Your one," he explains, "had been something of a scallywag back then. But you see, she was reformed in our Mary's laundry. She became a well-married woman."

The Butter Urn Resurrection

For "Brianna," who entrusted her story to me, and for her mother,
"Eileen," who died at the Sisters of Our Lady of Charity of the
Refuge's Magdalen Asylum, High Park, Dublin.

Prostitutes are made, not born.
Rain is throwing through her voice.
Eileen was a destroyed person.

Eileen, imagine—your daughter's body
twice the age of your own given up
after the three kids and old Conor.

Brianna no longer the balloon-eyed lamb
you stored in oak, in the safe embrace
of a butter urn while you decamped

for the razz of town, desperate
to be lost in the happiness of dance,
of abandon and redress and surfeit

of euphoria in fleshy rhythm.
They say she could make a fiddle talk.
Her rain thrashes like a brinewind.

Drifts of roast poultry, potatoes
in the cooker, and veg warm through
the parlor and fatten with the pathos.

Everything in this home yields open.
For years, I've wondered if I was a daughter
of rape. But that's not how I see him.

Da was a lovely, a mild man,
cracked in-love (Jameson-mended).
Eileen'd not have him, her own husband.

In the end, he forced it, and she made him pay.
How figurative that sounds! Who would
guess it tradition, Eileen, or your means to inveigh

against the act that had whipped the adult
you had not become out of chrysalis:
before Conor, your father's assaults

compensated with scraps of cash:
sex as conflict, waged in your verdure.
Where his body lay, the field grew black.

Lover is a word that sways from the earth.
Hard luck on Conor—farmer nearly
old as your father—his holding cursed

by his in-law's piseog
of trespass and desecration.
Lover for you: a handful of straw

letters burning, swollen with smoke.
Like *child*, like *trust*, like *moral* or *whore*.
What do words mean when they come to you broke?

That last day you tucked in the beams
of the churn your daughter, you, oh you
too stayed fastened in the womb-dream

dark of the wood, its solid world
far from harm. Just the concept,
the body of you (framework of a girl

you couldn't outgrow) went vanishing.
What can we offer the next events?
Can we surprise, damage, bring

ourselves to grieve that the Legion of Mary
found, after two years of lane,
that shell diluvian—its berry-

ripe insides tumbling from procedure,
from a last attempt to halt recurrence?
There was nowhere, then, for your return;

no prop save cement and despondence
to nest the bulb of a new head.
This time, your flesh pled *rinse*

it all. Please, I have had enough.
Your reservoirs, dams, held-back
waters rushed, red as love.

In the cradle of her parlor, your daughter cries
in smashing floods. Bursts, my God—
Wasn't it a blessing that she died?

Passion of rain. There is so much here
to drench us and surely, no surface?
Narrative of gulf, of pour. . . .

Brianna cautions: in this case, at least
the convent you ended up in, the walls
that closed around your last few weeks,

meant not just left to bleed. Her breath
hitching, she has you parented at last:
She'll always be a child, bless

her, poor thing. She has made me
a mother again—so vulnerable.
Of those writ off as bad, *So many*

Eileens—God! Can't we be small-
minded and judgmental? Self-congratulating Christians.
When did we forget: history is people?

Her sobs fight between us,
gutting distance. Her hand, my own.
Trust now ferocious—

a way to forgive all the black
absences, the not doing, the
catacombs of waste and wrack.

Some spit or burble from the pan
puts flurry in her and she's gone:
tending the veg, bathing the hen.

Soon, there is dinner in an alcove
off the kitchen—bulgy globe
of timber slats, glass light, a sea of photos. . . .

The heart, I think, must look like this.
I'd hate to imagine I won't see you again,
after everything. What is left but *Yes*

and the walking away, and the station?
Christ, where do I go from here?
To whom—shaking, wound-wet, impatient

to cry like light: *there is proof of salvation?*

So Long Imagined

In 1993, the Sisters of Our Lady of Charity of the Refuge exhumed the bodies of 155 "Magdalens" buried on the grounds of High Park Convent, Dublin, in order to sell off land. Spokespeople indicated the money was needed to help pay for new housing and care facilities for women still living with the nuns. The exhumations, cremations (a mortal sin for Catholics during the lifetimes of most of the deceased), and reinterments in a communal grave in Glasnevin Cemetery spurred a storm of media attention and public outrage that decried them as disrespectful of the dead and the categorically devalued. These events played a key role in bringing the Magdalen laundries into the light of public discourse.

Through months compassed with little more than hospital
corridors and the albatross of a body giving out,
she absorbs the acrid press like winter. Decides

the prevalence of machinery—now, the unflappable
sugar drip through dawn, the heat vent's rude
white-noising, the tele a-prate in attempt to be company—
illustrates: *Care is a flawed negotiation:*

apparatus, cogs, objective, revolution. (Is it, though,
the province of maintenance or action? Who can tell?)

She wonders if it all means she must reunderstand
the work, her life spent much in the grip of the middle-century, as less
service than administration.
                              But it had been real—the dying
to the self—surrender of children, dissimilitude, the good earth
of the gaze that follows a kiss, the fields at home, the village. . . .

It had been real—renunciation opening like a bowl
in the heart, wanting her to offer, and to hold.

And long before, the farm convincing her
it's good neighboring
that keeps the corn from rotting on the stalk.

There had been, as well, that irresistible sense of
revelation in the margin, its call
bare and ruptured as a bird's, female.

Now, there is simply the white space of the sickroom,
taking what is said, the media and the condemnations.

There is, she thinks, still a sweeping
lack of accountability, still a lack
of imagination. No one, it seems, conceives
of the younger sisters: *Fallen women! What
a desperate phrase! Who among us isn't fallen?*

Does no one hear the cranking?
The kick and wheel of the machine?

"Medieval" sums an RTE weatherwoman,
wringing the *eval* as the collective shifts
attention from feature piece to cold-front. "Just
unbelievable." On the flip side of the screen, sole-white
hospital sheets ache their patient, snow to bone.

She applies the rub of syllogism: *They overlook that
we are daughters, and daughters are products
of homes.* (Kick, and the wheel around.)

? *Care
is a flawed negotiation.*

                    But it had been real—

the wound
and the recognition

the current
and the spoiled pool

the red cry

the wild white moon
of the scar

And too—

the shadow thrown by the light.

Every day of those years, she had offered
the Magnificat, *My soul magnifies the Lord,*
in honor of an intercessor. *He has scattered
the proud in the imagination of their hearts.*

So much sundered. Could it all return
to pride? To too much love of—

What was it, she wonders, *that we all so long imagined?*

World View

One having crossed an ocean, with its cod and industry and rocking
    dark that moved her toward no one in particular,
two women sit in the trim side room of a home.

She does not yet know why she's here, except generally, as the older
    woman has not revealed more on why she called about the
    newspaper letter.
The younger has come today by three-hour train.

She is perched on a sofa two feet from the older, who is only so much
    older.
Does not know this woman is about to say, *My mother's father would molest,
    then pay her.*

Does not know that in a moment, the home will be broken and she will
    be touching the hand of this woman, who will be saying *prostitute*,
    after *finally my father forced her, my father loved her*, before *backstreet*, and
    hemorrhage, and *Magdalen asylum*.
The child whose words those are has no reason to entrust them, to tell
    her—poet

from elsewhere, miles and years—and does not know
how this girl will want to give the child candlewood, and a picture of
    rain on the papery petals of a quince, and the quince.

That when she leaves, having been fed roast chicken, potatoes, and
    turnips in the breakfast room,
this girl will buy something—anything—at the station to mark this,
    buys a necklace: a cold and milk-blue moonstone, an eternity
    knot.

Body Sonnets
VIII. The Magdalen

Cresting the gradual stairs in the Museo del Duomo,
you come to the Maddalena, who is nearly a river
of hair. Her clothes, if they be clothes, Donatello
has ragged to tresses that leave her only more bare—
snaking the bight of her thigh's line, giving
rib into hip—in their tumbling watery upset.
How it engulfs her, how it falls and falls, this living
hair—this impression of restraint unkept.
How right, you think, knowing she simply caved
to abandon in that moment when she knelt
and wept. Standing, she looks not beautiful or saved
but tender, wretched, aching with all she has felt.
Supplication is want. Is this, you wonder,
what we feel before the devils go, or after?

Notes

Foreword

Ireland's first Magdalen asylum opened in Dublin in 1767. This was the Magdalen Asylum in Leeson Street, established by the Protestant philanthropist Lady Arabella Denny. It was modeled on an existing institution in England. Catholic-run Magdalen asylums were not unique to Ireland either, and both the Good Shepherd sisters and Sisters of Our Lady of Charity of the Refuge originally came to Ireland from France, where their mission was also the reclamation of "fallen" women. In addition to Ireland, England, and France, countries such as Scotland, the United States (in cities such as New York, Philadelphia, Boston, and San Francisco), Australia, Canada, and elsewhere also contained Magdalen institutions.

The 10 convent laundries referred to are the following:

In or near Dublin:

St. Mary's Asylum, High Park, Drumcondra, Sisters of Our Lady of Charity of the Refuge (the largest in Ireland, room for approx. 200)

Magdalen Asylum, formerly St. Mary's Penitents' Retreat, Lower Gloucester Street (now Sean McDermott Street), Dublin, Sisters of Our Lady of Charity of the Refuge

St. Mary Magdalen Asylum, Donnybrook, Irish Sisters of Charity

St. Patrick's Refuge, Dun Laoghaire, Sisters of Mercy

Cork:

Good Shepherd Magdalen Asylum, Sunday's Well

St. Mary Magdalen's Asylum, Irish Sisters of Charity

Galway:

Galway Magdalen Asylum, Sisters of Mercy

Limerick:

Good Shepherd Magdalen Asylum, Limerick

New Ross:

Good Shepherd Magdalen Asylum, New Ross

Waterford:

Good Shepherd Magdalen Asylum, Waterford

Northern counties also contained Magdalen asylums, including a large Good Shepherd institution in Belfast.

Historians such as Maria Luddy and Frances Finnegan have analyzed the archives of the convent Magdalen asylums from the nineteenth century, and the scholarship of such historians offers available statistical and other information on religious-run Magdalen institutions. James Smith's recent book also offers close examination of many issues.

A few developments seen in later decades of the twentieth century include, among others, the introduction of an unmarried mothers' allowance in 1973, advancing social attitudes and training for social care work, legislation on equal pay and employment opportunities for women in the 1970s, the "modernizing spirit" of Vatican II, and (as Finnegan points out) availability of the home washing machine. The last of Ireland's Magdalen laundries to close was Dublin's Gloucester Street laundry in 1996. In several places, however, communities of women who worked in the laundries remained living with the nuns.

The laundries began to gain visibility in 1992 with the acclaimed play *Eclipsed*. The play was written by Patricia Burke Brogan, a former novice with the Sisters of Mercy, who had briefly spent time supervising in the Galway Magdalen Asylum in the 1960s. The institutions then broke into broad consciousness in 1993, when the nuns at High Park convent exhumed the bodies of 155 "Magdalen" women to sell off land. This incited a blaze of public and media outrage, reignited later by documentary film testimony from women who had been confined in Magdalen institutions, and the laundries finally began to enter contemporary discussion.

The English-made Magdalen laundry documentary, *Witness: Sex in a Cold Climate* (1998), evoked great public response, and together with Scottish *Washing Away the Stain* (1993), French *Les Blanchisseuses de Magdalen* (1998), and an American *60 Minutes* segment (1999), gave vital voice to former laundry inmates. In 2002, Scottish filmmaker Peter Mullan's feature film *The Magdalene Sisters* premiered, winning the Golden Lion Award at the Venice Film Festival. Among other significant impacts, the movie drew a great deal of international attention to the laundries, dramatically increasing awareness outside of Ireland.

Women who remained in Magdalen laundries until they died are largely buried in communal grave plots. Until the developments and advocacy of the 1990s, these generally did not list individual names. Many women's real names are no longer known, as they were changed upon entry to the asylums.

Poems

"Amazing Grace:" In the last stanza of section one, "It is the grace of God that runs the refuge" is a quote from "St. Mary Magdalen's, Donnybrook, Dublin" (1941). So are the following statements: "Look at this placid, fair, old face. She has not a care in the world. . . . Perhaps of her own free will she came here to the quiet arms of Charity. Perhaps she was gently led here. . . . Fifty years, sixty years—proudly they count out the years of their service spent in laborious, prayerful days and nights of glad rest after labour." The title of section two is from Psalm 51:10. "The blood of Jesus Christ His Son cleanses us of all sin" is from I John 1:7. "Grace responds to the deepest yearnings of human freedom" is from the Catechism (2022). The last line is from Mark 15:34, translated as, "My God, My God, why have You forsaken Me?"

"Research Piece: 'sub rosa':" Definitions from Random House Webster's and American Heritage dictionaries.

"Falling Away, *a pathetic fallacy*:" The *Princeton Encyclopedia of Poetry and Poetics* defines "pathetic fallacy" as "the tendency of poets and painters to imbue the natural world with human feeling."

"Letters to a Girl on Leaving the Home:" People often equate Magdalen laundries with "mother and baby homes." These institutions were also run by female Catholic orders, but specifically for expectant, then post-birth unwed mothers. At varying lengths of time after giving birth, mothers were separated from their children, who were adopted, fostered out, or put into industrial schools. Some women were required to stay up to several years—during which they performed work that supported the running of the homes—before separation. Unlike Magdalen asylums, mother and baby homes received regular per capita funding from the state.

"Five Images of Bliss:" The italicized words are those of Co. Galway—born Christina Mulcahy, as featured in the documentary *Sex in a Cold Climate*. In the 1940s, Christina gave birth in a mother and baby home, after which her father refused to allow her to return to her family. She then spent three years in the Galway Magdalen home, run by the Sisters of Mercy, before escaping.

"Season's Greetings:" "Bunch-of-keys" is a vernacular name for cowslips (*Flora Britannica*).

"Research Piece: Correspondence from 'Mrs. Mahony':" "Mrs. Mahony" was kind enough to correspond with me at some length regarding her memories of growing up on Forster Street, Galway. The words of this poem are hers. The story of the young maid was shared with her by a friend. She clarified that she thought it unlikely that the girl would have remained in a laundry during pregnancy.

"Fragments of the Shattering Glass:" The pope's apology was made March 12, 2000, and sins against women was one of seven areas addressed. The fathers' actions described here are based on things said in *Sex in a Cold Climate* and *Les Blanchisseuses de Magdalen*. The fourteen-year-old referred to is Martha Cooney, one of the women featured in *Sex in a Cold Climate*.

"Her Last Immolation:" "It is all still written" refers to Article 41.2.1 of the 1937 Constitution of Éire: "In particular, the State recognizes that by her life within the home, woman gives to the State a support without which the common good cannot be achieved." Article 41.1.1 states: "The State recognizes the Family as the natural primary and fundamental unit group of Society, and as a moral institution possessing inalienable and imprescriptible rights, antecedent and superior to all positive law." Article 41.1.2: "The State, therefore, guarantees to protect the Family and its constitution and authority, as the necessary basis of social order and as indispensable to the welfare of the Nation and the State."

"Oh Rose—His Dark Secret Love:" When the perpetrator in the "Kilkenny Incest Case" was convicted in 1993, the maximum prison sentence for incest by a male was seven years, under the Punishment of Incest Act of 1908. The Criminal Justice Act of 1993 amended the maximum to twenty years. The "West of Ireland Farmer Case" involving the abuse of Sophia McColgan and her siblings was tried in 1995. That year, the Criminal Law (Incest Proceedings) Act of 1995 increased the maximum sentence for incest by a male to life imprisonment. These women courageously tell their stories in *The Kilkenny Incest Case* and *Sophia's Story*.

"Kimberlys on the Number Seventeen:" Kimberlys are a popular cookie or "biscuit" in Ireland.

"The Butter Urn Resurrection:" *Piseog* "is usually glossed 'charm,' 'spell,'or in the plural, 'superstition'" (Bourke, 73). One illustrative description speaks to a practice "of making a *piseog*, which is frequently a nest of hay or straw in which is placed a piece of rotting meat or rotten eggs or a used sanitary towel. This is then hidden on the land of the person one wishes to use it against. The logic of the belief is that as the piseog decays so will the good luck of the farmer" (Richard Breen, "The Ritual Expression of Inter-Household Relationships in Ireland," as quoted in Bourke, 92).

"So Long Imagined:" Originally, people understood there to have been 133 bodies exhumed from the grounds at High Park Convent. Ten years later, it emerged that while the initial exhumation license had been for 133 sets of remains, during disinterment, the undertakers discovered the bodies of an additional 22 women, of whom there had apparently been no record. "Renunciation of the pleasures of the flesh was an essential aspect of the 'dying to self' demanded by the religious life, and the sacrifice of life-long companionship and children which this entailed was often stressed" (Clear, 136). The exclamation about fallen women was made to me in discussion with an Irish Sister of Charity about Donnybrook. The Magnificat, Luke 1:46–55, is spoken by the Virgin Mary.

Acknowledgments

Very grateful acknowledgment is made to the following journals, in which these poems first appeared:

American Literary Review: "Body Sonnets, I. Credibility," "Body Sonnets, VIII. The Magdalen"

Chautauqua Literary Journal: "The Butter Urn Resurrection," "Kimberlys on the Number Seventeen"

CutThroat, A Journal of the Arts: "Oh Rose—His Dark Secret Love"

Perihelion: "The Glass Lake, "Letters to a Girl on Leaving the Home," "Wild Fuchsia," "Body Sonnets, II. Death of a Maiden," "Body Sonnets, V. Composition"

Spoon River Poetry Review: "The Magdalen Laundries," "Body Sonnets, VII. Escape"

TriQuarterly: "The Cloistering of Mary Norris," "Guarded"

Special thanks to the following editors at those journals: Susan Hahn, Susan Kelly DeWitt, Bruce Guernsey, Jill Gerard, Pam Uschuk and William Pitt Root, and the editorial team at *ALR*.

My deep and heartfelt appreciation to the United States Fulbright Program and its Irish counterpart, the Ireland-United States Commission for Educational Exchange, whose grants made possible the research and creation of this volume.

To Rita Dove, whose belief in and support for this work as the judge of the 2008 Akron Poetry Prize enabled it to indeed become a book—I am forever indebted, and overwhelmed with gratitude. My great and warmest thanks, as well, to Mary Biddinger and everyone at the University of Akron Press for their wonderful support for this book and their genuine partnership, which is so appreciated.

My gratitude to the Poetry Society of the United Kingdom, which commended "Body Sonnets, VIII. The Magdalen" in its National Poetry Competition, and to the Academy of American Poets and *Glimmer Train*, which honored "The Magdalen Laundries" with prizes. Thanks to the Bread Loaf Writers' Conference for a scholarship that helped with revising some of these poems.

Teachers of many things have provided valuable insights, guidance, and help. I would particularly like to thank Alan Williamson, Langdon Hammer, and Sandy McPherson for supporting this project at its birth.

This book would not have been possible without the unfailing and ever-heartening love, belief, and encouragement of my family, and in particular my parents, Ray and Nan Dilworth. Dad, Mom, Tim, Drew, Jen, Marianne, Aurora, Elena, Ryan, Clara, Katie, and Sofia—I love you all so much.

I am grateful, as well, for the encouragement of many dear friends, with special thanks to Em Greer and Bill Tessier, who were there with love from first to last. Additionally, living alone abroad, I was very fortunate that the friendship and help of a number of women made me feel much more "at home" than I might have, and I would especially like to thank Ellen Keane Cope, Mamo MacDonald, Moira Maguire, Jackie Ryan, Grainne Blair, Ann Leahy, Phil O'Neill, and Lynda Hughes.

I am wholly indebted for, inspired and moved by, the trust, assistance, and personal generosity extended to me by many people in Ireland during my work on these poems. Individuals with very different perspectives, experiences, stories, and insight spoke with me, or helped this work in some way. My great thanks for the support provided by Ailbhe Smyth and colleagues at the Women's Education Research and Resource Center at University College Dublin, the Centre for Social Care Research at Waterford Institute for Technology, and Rita Ann Higgins; also to Patrick Sammon of the Irish Fulbright Commission, for his very valuable assistance during the grant. Sincere gratitude to everyone who guided me to readings, issues, people, and more.

I would especially like to say how deeply I value and appreciate the personal openness shown in my conversations with Mary Norris, Josephine McCarthy, "Brianna," Bridget Schrompf, and many others. I am grateful that a member of all four religious orders that ran convent laundries met with me and shared thoughts. Special thanks for the time and perspectives of everyone listed at the end of this book, among others.

To the at-present still literally uncountable number of women who entered Magdalen asylums and had voices, experiences, possibilities, sometimes children, even names that became lost in the silences and years of the laundries—*I acknowledge you.*

Resources

The following resources were useful, among others, in learning more about, and gaining a sense of perspectives on, relevant issues.

Discussions with the Author:
"Brianna," daughter of "Eileen," who died at the Magdalen Asylum, High Park, Dublin.

Patricia Burke Brogan, author of *Eclipsed*, former novice with the Sisters of Mercy in the early 1960s, as which she briefly spent time supervising in the Galway Magdalen Asylum.

Joe Costello, TD, Labour Party, Central Dublin, worked with the Magdalen Memorial Committee.

Terry Fagan, North Inner City Folklore Project.

Bernadette Fahy, author of *Freedom of Angels*, assisted a friend in 1972 in "claiming out" her mother from the Good Shepherd Magdalen Asylum, Cork.

"Mrs. Mahony," resident of Galway and "Magdalen Terrace" throughout her youth.

Josephine McCarthy, Good Shepherd Magdalen Asylum, Cork, 1961–64.

Patricia McDonnell, Margo Kelly, and Blathnaid Ni Chinneide, co-founders of the Magdalen Memorial Committee. This is a citizen group that protested the High Park exhumations and lack of broad notice of the reinterment, organized a public memorial service, and advocated with government officials to secure the permanent memorial bench and plaque in St. Stephen's Green, Dublin. Patricia is an in-law of a woman who spent nineteen years in the Sisters of Mercy laundry, Dun Laoghaire; Margo is an adult adoptee, and Blathnaid a concerned citizen.

Declan McEntee, son of Ina McEntee, who was a paid outside worker in the Galway Magdalen home and who helped some women escape.

Mary Norris, Good Shepherd Magdalen Asylum, Cork, 1950–early 1953.

A representative of FAOISEAMH and a Presentation sister with the Conference of Religious of Ireland.

Bridget Schrompf, Good Shepherd Magdalen Asylum, Limerick, 1958–61.

A sister with the Good Shepherds, Waterford. At the time we met, a number of women were still living with these nuns.

A sister with the Irish Sisters of Charity, worked in the Donnybrook
    laundry for twenty years, from her entry to the order in the early
    1970s.
A sister with the Sisters of Mercy, in the administrative tier of the Western
    Province.
A sister with the Sisters of Our Lady of Charity of the Refuge, High Park,
    Dublin. At one time, superintendent of the laundry; joined the order
    mid-1940s. At the time we met, a number of women were still living
    with these nuns.
Two former inmates of the High Park industrial school, located on same
    grounds as the laundry; one also spent two weeks in the Gloucester
    Street laundry.
Phone and other conversations with many people.

Books and Articles:

Bourke, Angela. *The Burning of Bridget Cleary*. London: Pimlico, 1999.
Burke Brogan, Patricia. *Above the Waves Calligraphy*. Galway: Salmon
    Publishing Ltd., 1994.
——. *Eclipsed*. Galway: Salmon Publishing Ltd., 1994.
Clear, Caitriona. *Nuns in Nineteenth-Century Ireland*. Dublin: Gill and
    Macmillan, 1987.
Conlan-McKenna, Marita. *The Magdalen*. London: Bantam Books, 1999.
Cooney, John. *John Charles McQuaid, Ruler of Catholic Ireland*. Dublin: The
    O'Brien Press, 1999.
Doyle, Paddy. *The God Squad*. London: Corgi, 1989.
Drennan, Mary Phil. *You May Talk Now!* Cork: On Stream Publications,
    1994.
Fahy, Bernadette. *Freedom of Angels: Surviving Goldenbridge Orphanage*. Dublin:
    The O'Brien Press, 1999.
Finnegan, Frances. *Do Penance or Perish: A Study of Magdalen Asylums in Ireland*.
    Piltown: Congrave Press, 2001.
Goulding, June. *The Light in the Window*. Dublin: Poolbeg Press, 1999.
Guilbride, Alexis. "I Went Away in Silence: a Study of Infanticide in
    Ireland from 1925 to 1957." Unpublished M.A. Thesis, University
    College Dublin, 1994.
Haskins, Susan. *Mary Magdalen, Myth and Metaphor*. New York: Riverhead
    Books, 1993.
Hoff, Joan, and Moureen Coulter, eds. *Irish Women's Voices: Past and Present*, a
    publication of the *Journal of Women's History*. Bloomington: Indiana
    University Press, 1995.

Inglis, Tom. *Moral Monopoly: The Catholic Church in Modern Irish Society*. Dublin: Gill & Macmillan, 1987.

Luddy, Maria. "'Behaved Very Ill': Rescue Work and Magdalen Asylums in the Nineteenth and Twentieth Centuries." In *Prostitution and Irish Society 1800–1940*, 76–123. Cambridge: Cambridge University Press, 2007.

———. "Prostitution and Rescue Work in Nineteenth-Century Ireland." In *Women Surviving: Studies in Irish Women's History in the 19th and 20th Centuries*, edited by Maria Luddy and Cliona Murphy, 51–84. Dublin: Poolbeg, 1989.

———. "Women and Charitable Organisations in Nineteenth-Century Ireland." *Women's Studies International Forum* 11, no. 4 (special issue on "Feminism in Ireland," Ailbhe Smyth, ed., 1988), 301–5.

———. *Women and Philanthropy in Nineteenth-Century Ireland*. Cambridge: Cambridge University Press, 1995.

———. *Women in Ireland, 1800–1918: A Documentary History*. Cork: Cork University Press, 1995.

MacCurtain, Margaret. "Godly Burden: Catholic Sisterhoods in 20th-Century Ireland." In *Gender and Sexuality in Modern Ireland*, edited by Anthony Bradley and Maryann Valiulis, 245–256. Amherst: University of Massachusetts Press, 1997.

———. "Towards an Appraisal of the Religious Image of Women." In *The Crane Bag Book of Irish Studies (1977–1981)*, edited by Mark P. Hederman and Richard Kearney, 539–43. Dublin: Blackwater Press, 1982.

Maguire, Moira. "The Changing Face of Catholic Ireland: Conservatism and Liberalism in the Ann Lovett and Kerry Babies Scandals." *Feminist Studies* 27, no. 2 (2001): 335–58.

Mahood, Linda. *The Magdalenes: Prostitution in the Nineteenth Century*. London: Routledge, 1990.

McElwee, C. Niall. "The Magdalen Debate: Reflections on Unbalanced Reporting." *Religious Life Review* 37, no. 191 (July/August 1998): 220–24.

McKay, Susan, with Sophia McColgan. *Sophia's Story*. Dublin: Gill & Macmillan, 1998.

McLoughlin, Dympna. "Women and Sexuality in Nineteenth Century Ireland." *The Irish Journal of Psychology* 15, nos. 2 & 3 (1994): 266–75.

Meehan, Paula. "The Statue of the Virgin at Granard Speaks" (poem). In *The Man Who Was Marked by Winter*, 40–42. Loughcrew/Oldcastle: Gallery Press, 1991.

Ni Chuilleanain, Eilean, ed. *Irish Women: Image and Achievement*. Dublin: Arlen House, 1985.

Norris, Mary. "Graves Row: Living in Slavery." *Kerry's Eye*, Oct. 30, 1997.

Rich, Adrienne. *What Is Found There: Notebooks on Poetry and Politics.* New York: W. W. Norton, 1993.

Robbins, Joseph. *The Lost Children: A Study of Charity Children in Ireland 1700–1900.* Dublin: Institute of Public Administration, 1980.

Smith, James. *Ireland's Magdalen Laundries and the Nation's Architecture of Containment.* Notre Dame: University of Notre Dame Press, 2007.

Widdess, J. D. H. *The Magdalen Asylum: 1766–1966.*

Wood, Kieron, with the victim in the Kilkenny Incest Case. *The Kilkenny Incest Case.* Dublin: Poolbeg, 1993.

Many articles from newspapers, including *An Phoblacht/Republican News, Evening Herald, Hot Press, Ireland on Sunday, The Irish Independent, The Irish Times, Sunday Business Post, Sunday Independent.*

Older Resources:

Atkinson, Sara. "The Penitent's Home." In *Mary Aikenhead: Her Life, Her Work, and Her Friends*, 466–73. Dublin, 1879.

Author of "The Christian Minister." *The Magdalen: A Tale of Real Life* (includes "The Magdalen's Hymn"). Dublin: P. D. Hardy, 1832.

Barrett, Rosa. "Homes for Fallen Women, or Penitentiaries." In *Guide to Dublin Charities*. Part III, 1–6. Dublin, 1884.

Butler, Beatrice Bayley. "Lady Arabella Denny, 1707–1792," *Dublin Historical Record,* vol. IX, no. I (Dec. 1946–Feb. 1947): 1–20.

Dodd, Rev. William. *An Account of the Rise, Progress and Present State of the Magdalen Charity.* London: W. Faden, 1761.

"A Letter to the Public on an Important Subject." Dublin: Printed for J. Sheppard, 1767.

The Magdalen Asylum, Leeson Street. Admissions Books for years 1767–68, 1828–43. Annual Reports 1937, 1954, 1972, 1974.

"The Magdalens of High Park." *The Irish Rosary*, vol. I, 1897: 176–84.

The Standard (an Irish organ of Catholic opinion), 1935, 1940.

"The Vices of To-Day, Morals of a Country, The Ramparts of the Faith." *Irish Independent*, March 14, 1934.

"St. Mary Magdalen's, Donnybrook, Dublin." In *The Irish Sisters of Charity*, as reprinted from *St. Anthony's Annals*. 26–30. Dublin: The Anthonian Press, 1941.

Documentaries, Television and Radio Broadcasts, Films:

Dear Daughter. Directed by Louis Lentin. Crescendo Concepts, 1996.

Hush-a-Bye Baby. Written by Margo Harkin and Stephanie English. Directed by Margo Harkin. Derry Film and Video Workshop, 1990.

Kenny Live segment on the Magdalen laundries. RTE, Sept. 25, 1993.

Les Blanchiseusses de Magdalen. Nicolas Glimois and Christophe Weber. France 3/Sunset Presse, 1998.

"The Magdalen Laundries," *60 Minutes* segment with Steve Kroft. CBS News, 1999.

"The Magdalen Laundry." Produced by Julian Vignoles. RTE Radio, 1992.

The Magdalene Sisters. Written and directed by Peter Mullan. A PFP Film Production in association with Temple Films, 2002.

States of Fear. Written, directed, and produced by Mary Raftery. RTE, 1999.

Washing Away the Stain. Directed by Andrea Miller and Sarah Barclay. BBC 2 Scotland, 1993.

Witness: Sex in a Cold Climate. Produced by Steven Humphries. Testimony Films for Channel 4, 1998.

Roger Mitchell, *Half/Mask*
Alison Pelegrin, *Big Muddy River of Stars*
Jeff Gundy, *Spoken among the Trees*
Brian Brodeur, *Other Latitudes*
William Greenway, *Everywhere at Once*
Heather Derr-Smith, *The Bride Minaret*
John Gallaher, *Map of the Folded World*
John Minczeski, *A Letter to Serafin*
Rachel Dilworth, *The Wild Rose Asylum: Poems of the Magdalen Laundries of Ireland*